More of
The
World's Best
Jewish Jokes

Ben Eliezer

More of The World's Best Jewish Jokes

Illustrations by Menachem Gueffen

ANGUS
& ROBERTSON
PUBLISHERS

By the same author:
THE WORLD'S BEST JEWISH JOKES

To my wife

ANGUS & ROBERTSON PUBLISHERS

Unit 4, Eden Park, 31 Waterloo Road,
North Ryde, NSW, Australia 2113, and
16 Golden Square, London W1R 4BN,
United Kingdom

First published in Australia by
Angus & Robertson Publishers in 1985
First published in the United Kingdom by
Angus & Robertson (UK) Ltd in 1985
Reprinted 1985, 1988

The British Library Cataloguing in
Publication Data.

Eliezer, Ben
  More of the World's Best Jewish Jokes

  1. Jews – Anecdotes, facetiae, satire, etc.
  2. English wit and humour
  I. Title
  828'.02 PN6231.J5
  ISBN 0-207-15235-7

Reproduced printed and bound in Great Britain by
Hazell Watson & Viney Limited

Introduction

In the days of *Jaws II* and *Godfather II*, all successes carry within them the seeds of a sequel. Thus *The World's Best Jewish Jokes* had a few pages at the back optimistically inviting readers to send in their favourites for the sequel — the volume you now hold in your hands. To these readers, some of whose jokes I have used, I offer my thanks: Esmond Towers, David Goulding, D. W. Forecast (who wrote pointing out that he wasn't a Jew — but was saving up to be one) and Douglas Jaggers. My thanks also to Steven Pincus, Eve Pollard, James Hazeldine and many other friends.

What does a French woman say when she's making love?

"Ah! C'est merveilleux!"

An Italian woman?

"Ah! Oo! Che Meravigliosa!"

A Jewish woman?

"Sam! The ceiling needs painting!"

Ginsberg goes to Harrods. "I want to buy my wife a really nice fountain pen for her birthday."

"Ah!" said the sales assistant, "that will be a nice surprise."

"It certainly will. She's expecting a mink coat!"

A bishop and a vicar and a rabbi were engaged in a deep theological discussion on the nature of miracles.

"Well," said the bishop, "I have personal experience of a miracle. I took some of my flock walking in the Alps, and all of a sudden there was a fearsome avalanche and all of my friends were buried. A huge rock fall was just about to crash on my head when I prayed to God and suddenly the avalanche stopped, the sun came out and I was saved."

"Wonderful! Amazing!" agreed the other two.

"Well," said the vicar, "I was on a small ferry boat in the South China Sea with some of my faithful flock when suddenly there was a terrible storm and the boat sank and everyone was drowned. I prayed to God and suddenly found a lifebelt and a raft, and the storm ended and I was rescued."

"Well," said the rabbi, "that was remarkable! But I have an even more dramatic tale to tell. I was returning from Synagogue service on the Sabbath day when, as you both know, Jews are not allowed to handle money of any kind. Anyway, by the side of the road I saw a small, smart case. I opened it up and it was full of £50 notes. I couldn't touch it! What a tragedy! So I prayed to God, and guess what? Suddenly it was Wednesday!"

G insberg never pays his bills and is seen bargaining with a supplier.

"Hey, Ginsberg," Goldberg asks him, "why are you knocking that man's prices down. You're never going to pay him anyway."

"Listen," answers Ginsberg, "he's a nice chap. I just want to keep down his losses!"

Old Mr Levy knocked at the door of the sperm bank. A nurse came to the door. "Well, Sir? What can I do for you?"

"Well, I'd like to make a contribution."

"Aren't you a bit old, Sir?" asked the nurse.

"Not at all," protested Mr Levy, beating his chest. "I may be 80 years old but I'm as fit as a fiddle."

So the nurse let him in, gave him a covered jar and told him to go behind a curtained-off closet to make a deposit.

An hour passed, then two hours. Eventually the doctor came by. "Well nurse, how did old Mr Levy do?"

"Goodness me, I've forgotten all about him." She stood outside Mr Levy's closet and said, "Well Mr Levy, how are you doing?"

"Not so well," confessed the old man. "I've tried with my left hand — nothing! I've tried with my right hand — nothing! I've tried with both hands — but I still can't get the top off the jar!"

J ust after the Six Day War, President Johnson rang Golda Meir, the Israeli Prime Minister.

"Say, Golda! I'm having trouble in Vietnam, will you let me have General Dayan? In return you can have any two of our generals."

Golda consults her cabinet. She rings back. "O.K., Mr President! You can have Dayan. And the two generals we want are General Motors and General Electric!"

J oe Levy goes into a shop. "Excuse me! I'll have a pair of black shoelaces."

"Sorry. I don't sell them. I only sell salt."

Levy looks around. "Goodness me! Hundreds of sacks of salt. You must sell a lot of salt!"

"Me? Nah! I don't sell any salt! But the guy I buy from — wow! Can he sell salt!"

A man started to tell a joke at a party: "Two old Jews were on their way…"

Suddenly he was interrupted by a sensitive guest. "Why do so many jokes begin with Jews?"

"Oh, I'm sorry," apologised the story teller, "I'll start again. Two old Chinese men were on their way to the synagogue to see the rabbi…"

What a disaster!
Ginsberg spent the whole of Yom Kippur with a magnificent whore. He had met the long-legged voluptuous blonde at a trade reception and spent three days at a hotel with her. About 6.00 pm on the evening of Yom Kippur, all bleary-eyed in bed, he sat up suddenly with a yell. "Mine God! What have I done! Oy! It's Yom Kippur!" He leapt from bed, got dressed in a trice, peeled of a wad of big notes from his wallet, kissed the girl goodbye and fled. On his way home he passed a United Synagogue (very orthodox). He burst in, cornered the rabbi, and blurted out: "Rabbi! It's terrible! I missed Yom Kippur! I completely forgot."

"You forgot Yom Kippur! Oy veh! How?"

"I-I-I-oh God! — I was with a-a-woman."

"A woman? Who? Your mother? Your wife?"

"No. No, a-a-bad, a professional, a-a-tart."

"What!? On Yom Kippur?"

"Yes, Rabbi! What can I do to repent?"

"My God! I have to think about it, consult my colleagues, summon the Rabbinical Court. But first you must go home, wear sackcloth, cover yourself in ashes and eat nothing for a week. Come back and see me in a week and I'll have your punishment worked out."

Ginsberg crept out of the synagogue utterly crestfallen. What shame! On his way he passed a Liberal Synagogue and, on an impulse, went inside. The rabbi was sitting with his feet up, filing his nails. Ginsberg rushed up to him. "Rabbi! I must tell you, I missed Yom Kippur!"

"What? you missed Yom Kippur. Serious! How did you do it?"

"I was with a woman," moaned Ginsberg.

"Really? Tell me about her."

"She was a tall voluptuous blonde, not my wife, not my fiancée, she was a-a-whore! What can I do?"

"Well, I'll have to consult my colleagues, but for a start you'd better skip lunch..."

"Skip lunch?" gasped Ginsberg. "But the rabbi at United Synagogue told me I had to fast a whole week — and that's just for starters!"

"United Synagogue? United Synagogue? What do they know about sex?"

Hitler was infuriated by the anti-Nazi jokes that were popular in Germany as soon as he came to power. He issued an order to the Gestapo: "Find out who's responsible and bring him to me!"

So a Jewish comedian, Yossel von Goldbloom, was dragged into the Führer's presence.

Hitler roared: "Did you invent the one about me and the ass?"

"Yes," admitted Goldbloom.

"What about the one about me and the swine?"

"Yes, me too," nodded Goldbloom.

"And the one that says the day I die will be a Jewish holiday?"

"That too, I'm afraid," confessed Goldbloom.

"You pig of a Jew!" screamed Hitler. "Don't you realise I'm the Führer of the Third Reich — a great empire that will last a thousand years?"

"Ha! Ha!" shrieked Goldbloom, falling all over the place, "that's wonderful! But you can't blame me for that one — I never heard it before!"

A very orthodox Talmud student returns home to Vilna after years in America.

"Tell me," said his mother, "what happened to your beard?"

"No-one wears beards in Los Angeles, I shaved it off."

"You still go to Synagogue every day!"

"That's impossible in America."

"You go on the Sabbath at least!"

"Mama, people work on Saturday in America."

"Do you go then on Yom Kippur at least?"

"It so happened I was out of town that day, but I did skip lunch."

"Oy veh! Tell me, are you still circumcised?"

A queue for food outside a Moscow grocery.
The Manager comes out: "The next delivery isn't due till later and there won't be enough for everyone anyway so will all the Jews please go home."

The Jews shuffle off while the others smile smugly.

Two hours later the manager comes out again. "The delivery has been delayed again so will all who aren't Communist Party members please go home."

Eventually three hours later the manager appears again. "There won't be any delivery today after all," he announces, "so everyone can go home."

As they're leaving for home, one shopper says to the other: "Those damned Jews, how is it they always get special treatment?"

A Russian, a Hungarian and a Jew were sentenced to death for spying in Moscow.

"Scatter my ashes over Lenin's grave", begged the Russian.

"Scatter my ashes over Rakosi's grave," begged the Hungarian.

"Scatter my ashes over Gorbachov's grave!" begged the Jew.

"Idiot Jew! Don't you realise that Gorbachov isn't dead?"

"O.K.!" said the Jew, "so I'll wait!"

S ir Moses Montefiore, a famous Jewish philanthropist in Victorian England, was sitting next to an anti-Semitic nobleman at dinner.

"Just been to Japan," barked the Duke, "interesting country. No pigs and no Jews."

"Then you and I, my Lord, should go there at once. Then it would have one of each."

I t is said that the eighteenth century Jewish thinker, Moses Mendelssohn, was walking down a Berlin street when bumped into by a Prussian officer.

"Swine!" shouted the officer.

"Mendelssohn!" replied the Jew, bowing low.

A Jew from Odessa was sitting in the same compartment as a Czarist Russian officer who had a pig with him.

To annoy the Jew, the officer kept calling the pig Moishe. "Moishe! Moishe! Keep still! Come here!" This went on all the way to Kiev.

Eventually the Jew got fed up and said: "You know, Captain, it's a great shame your pig has a Jewish name."

"Now why is that, Jew?" smirked the officer.

"Well, otherwise it could have become an officer in the Czar's army."

Mendel Rosenbaum from Vienna decides to emigrate just before the Nazi takeover of 1938. He goes to the travel agent who scans the globe looking for a country that would take him. One country requires a work permit, another requires a resident guarantor, others won't take any immigrants, others have minimum financial requirements.

"Haven't you got a different globe?" asks Rosenbaum.

So Mendel tries the American Embassy as a last resort. But America is swamped with refugees.

"I'm afraid our quotas are full," declares the consul. "Come back in ten years."

"Hmm," mutters Mendel, "morning or afternoon?"

J ust after the Six Day War, a TV interviewer asked Moshe Dayan, "Tell me, General, how did you finish the war in only six days?"

"Well, we only had the tanks on a week's approval!"

G insberg returned home from a trip abroad on business to find out that his wife had been unfaithful. Very upset, he interrogated his wife.

"Was it that dung heap, Goldberg?"

"No."

"Was it that pile of filth, Feigenbaum?"

"No."

"Was it that swine Morrie Levy?"

"No."

Finally Ginsberg exploded. "What's the matter with my friends? Not good enough for you?"

A German priest is pleading with Hitler to spare the Jews. "I'll tell you why you shouldn't harm them — because they're so smart."

"Smart?" says our Adolf. "Who says they're smart?"

"Come with me. I'll show you." So the priest took Hitler to a little shop run by Mr Isaacson.

"Mr Isaacson," says the priest, "we're looking for a left-handed beer mug. Do you have one?"

"Sure," says Isaacson, and fetches one from the back of the store.

The priest turns to Hitler. "See what I mean?"

"What's so smart about that?" Hitler says. "He happened to have one in stock."

A Rabbi hears a knock at his front door, puts his head out of the window and shouts:

"Hello there! Who is it?"

"I'm a Jehovah's Witness," came back the voice.

"Good," answered the Rabbi, "tell him I hope he wins his case."

T he Jews of Chelm were considered stupid and therefore served as the butts for hundreds of jokes for other Jews. (In the same way every group picks on another to tell "stupid" jokes about: the Americans pick on the Poles, the French on the Belgians, the British on the Irish, the Irish on the people from County Kerry, etc.)

The rabbi from Chelm goes for a few days to visit Omsk and gets talking with the shamus (the caretaker, or beadle of the local synagogue). "You want to hear a riddle?" asks the shamus.

"Of course!" says the rabbi from Chelm.

"Right, listen carefully. Who is my mother's son but is not my brother?"

The rabbi is perplexed and cannot work it out.

"I give up," he says.

"It's me, of course," says the shamus, in triumph.

The rabbi couldn't wait to get back to Chelm and tell everyone this marvellous riddle.

He gathers the whole town together in the synagogue after the Sabbath prayers.

"Who is my mother's son but is not my brother?" he asks triumphantly.

There is much whispering and shaking of heads. But nobody can solve it. Eventually they ask the rabbi to tell them the answer.

"Why! It's the shamus from Omsk, of course!"

Abie the butcher is walking down Chelm's main street. Suddenly a man leaps at him and slaps his face. "Ya, Yossel! That's for you," he shouts. But to his surprise, Abie just smiles.

"So! Yossel! You're laughing! I'll hit you again!"

"Ha! Ha!" laughs Abie, "the joke's on you. I'm not Yossel!"

"Why is it, Rabbi," asked a wise old man of Chelm, "that if you drop a buttered slice of toast, it always falls on the buttered side?"

"We'll see," answered the rabbi, and he went into the kitchen, buttered a slice of toast and dropped it on the floor.

"Well" said the rabbi, "it fell on the other side."

"Mmm, you must have buttered the wrong side."

T he railway at last came to Chelm.

"Do you realise," Yossel told the rabbi, "that you can leave Chelm at seven o'clock at night and be in Tarnopol at midnight."

"So who wants to be in Tarnopol at midnight?"

T he tax inspector visited Chelm.

"I don't understand this tax business," said Abie to Shmulik. "Why does the Grand Duke need my roubles when he can print as many as he likes?"

"Well, Abie," said Shmulik, "think of it this way. Every time someone does a good deed, God creates an angel. He could make as many angels as he wants, but he wants one from *you* because he wants your good deed. In the same way, the Grand Duke wants *your* rouble."

T wo men from Chelm were going to see the rabbi when it started raining.

"Shmulik, put up your umbrella, it's raining."

"I can't, Mendel, it's got holes in it."

"Holes in it? Then why did you bring it with you?"

"I didn't think it would rain."

S hmulik goes to the post office with a parcel for his mother in Chelm.

"The parcel's too heavy," the clerk tells him. "Put on more stamps."

"And if I put on more stamps," asks Shmulik in amazement, "will it get lighter?"

The people of Chelm were terrible worriers. They even worried about how much they worried. So the mayor and rabbi appointed Itzik the candle maker to do all the worrying for the people of Chelm, and for this he would earn four roubles a week. But the scheme didn't work because Itzik went home to Beckie and said, "Wonderful! I've got four roubles a week. We've got nothing to worry about."

I f it takes three Irishmen to change a light bulb (one to hold the bulb and two to turn the room) and four Californians (one to change it, three to share the experience), how may Jewish mothers does it take to change a light bulb?

None. "Don't worry about me, I'll sit in the dark."

G oldberg and Ginsberg had been partners for years, but Goldberg had suddenly been taken ill and was on his deathbed. Ginsberg was with him and they started to reminisce about the good old days.

"My friend," said Goldberg in a quavering voice, "I have something terrible to confess. That year when we lost all that money and, you had to sell your house? I stole £50,000 from the company. Remember your new design for a raincoat that suddenly was all over town before we could go into production? It was me! I sold your drawings to Lefkowitz. You remember losing £10,000 from the office safe…"

"Don't worry! Don't worry, Goldberg!"

"Tell me! How come you're so forgiving?" asked the dying Goldberg.

"It's all O.K. now. It was me who poisoned you!"

"**I** 'm afraid you're going to need a lot of treatment and the fee will be $200 dollars," said Dr Carruthers to the unfortunate Goldberg.

"Doctor, I'm not a wealthy man and business is terrible!"

"O.K., then I'll make it $125!"

"Doctor, give me a break! I have three children to support!"

"O.K.! O.K.!" sighed the doctor, "I'll make it $75!"

"Doctor," pleaded Goldberg, "couldn't you make it a little less? I have my old mother who lives with me and I only work three days a week!"

"O.K! O.K.! I'll make it $50! But tell me, why do you come to me? I'm the most expensive specialist in New York!"

"When it comes to my health," said Goldberg, "money is no object!"

Yossel sat next to Shmulik at the back of the Synagogue. Every five minutes Shmulik shuffled his feet and winced in pain.

"What's the matter Shmulik?" whispered Yossel.

"It's my feet! They're killing me. My shoes are too small."

"Why do you wear shoes that are too small?"

"Ach! Two weeks ago I lost my job. My wife Sadie complains of rheumatism all day long and won't let me get near her. I can't pay the bills. My son Abie has abandoned his studies and it cost me my life savings already to put him into university and my daughter's run off with a goy. But when I take my shoes off, life seems wonderful!"

G insberg meets Goldberg.
"I've got a bargain for you!" says Ginsberg. "an elephant for only £50."

"You're crazy!" yells Goldberg, "I've got a wife and five children in two small rooms on the eighth floor!"

"O.K., you win," replies Ginsberg. "You can have two for £70."

"Right! Now you're talking."

A famous art critic called in on Ivor Dalrymple (formerly Feigenbaum) who had a great collection of pictures, including six remarkable Raphaels. The critic was astonished to see that the name Raphael, normally signed on the bottom right-hand corner of the picture (Rafaello) had been replaced by the name Rebecca.

"Why on earth are the pictures signed Rebecca?" queried the astonished art critic.

"Ah! That's because I put them in my wife's name."

Moishe Pitzky joins the Royal Marine Commandos. On the first night of training the bugle sounded reveille at three o'clock in the morning.

The sergeant kicked the recruits out of bed and made them stand to attention, naked, in the freezing cold.

The sergeant went up to the first man, punched him in the teeth, kicked him in the belly and beat his penis with a truncheon.

"Did that hurt?" yelled the sergeant.

"No!" yelled back the recruit.

"Why?" screamed the sergeant.

"Because I'm a Royal Marine Commando."

The sergeant went to the next man, kneed him in the groin, thumped him in the ear and punched his penis.

"Did that hurt?"

"No Sir!"

"Why?"

"Because I'm a Royal Marine Commando!"

This happened all the way down the line until he got to Moishe. He gave him an uppercut to the jaw, a kick in the shin and a great punch to the penis.

"Did that hurt?" yelled the sergeant.

"No!" yelled back Moishe.

"And why?" screamed the sergeant.

"Because it belongs to the man behind," answered Moishe.

G insberg finally had a mental breakdown and was admitted to a special hospital for the insane. He insisted on kosher food. They offered him a "meals on wheels" take out service but he insisted on eating in the canteen with the other patients, but his food had to be kosher. After much hassle and expense, the hospital finally laid on kosher food for Ginsberg, their only Jewish resident.

After a few weeks, the chief Psychiatrist was walking about the restaurant and saw Ginsberg eating a big plate of ham and eggs and drinking a glass of milk.

"But Ginsberg!" protested the doctor, "I thought you only ate kosher food!"

"Ah! Doctor! You've forgotten! I'm meshuggah!" (mad)

G insberg came home unexpectedly and found his wife in bed with Goldberg.

"What on earth are you doing?" yelled Ginsberg.

"See," said his wife to Goldberg, "I told you he was stupid."

M oishe Levich Finkelstein, a tailor from a small Ukrainian village, applies for membership of the Russian Communist party in Kiev.

"Who was Karl Marx?" asks the commissar.

"Never heard of him."

"Joseph Vissarionovitch Stalin?"

"Never met him."

"Who was Vladimir Ilyich Lenin?"

"Can't say I recall the name."

"Are you taking us for idiots?"

"Not for one moment, Comrade. Do you know Yossel Feigenbaum?"

"No."

"Do you know Mendele Levinsky?"

"Never heard of him!"

"Do you know Shpilkey Beazly?"

"I don't know who you're talking about!"

"Well," says Finkelstein, "that's the way it is. You have your friends and I have mine."

Why are there no golf courses in Israel?
The country's too small. One good drive could lead to a war.

(Note for my serious readers: there *is* a golf course in Israel. Sure, it's by the sea.)

Lord Rothschild was travelling through the poor East End of London on the way to his bank in the city. He stopped for a cup of tea at Sam Levy's café in Whitechapel. He was astonished at the bill. "Five pounds for one cup of tea? Is tea so rare?"

"No," replied Sam, "but Rothschilds are!"

G oldberg lost his wallet at his nephew's bar-mitzvah celebration.

"Sorry to disturb the celebrations," he announced, standing on a chair, "but I just lost my wallet with $500 in it. I offer a reward of $50 to anyone who finds it and returns it to me!"

Ginsberg shouted from the back: "And I offer $75!"

S quadron Leader "Buffy" Feigenbaum was shot down over Cario during the War of Attrition between Israel and Egypt. Badly injured, he was taken to a top Egyptian hospital. There he was examined by General Ibrahim-al-Fawzi, surgeon-general of the Egyptian army.

"My dear Squadron Leader," announced the general, "I'm afraid we are going to have to remove your left leg."

"Oh dear!," said Feigenbaum. "But perhaps you would be kind enough to do me a personal favour. Would you on your next bombing mission over Israel please drop the leg on my beloved country?"

"Dear fellow officer," responded the general, "I'd be delighted."

So Feigenbaum lost his left leg and the Egyptian airforce dropped it over Israel.

Two weeks later the surgeon-general again approached Feigenbaum's bed.

"I'm afraid I have more bad news. We have to amputate your right arm."

"Oh dear!" Feigenbaum was most upset. "But perhaps you'd drop it over Israel again."

Ten days later the general informed the Israeli pilot that he'd have to remove his right leg and again, at Feigenbaum's request, it was dropped over Israel.

Three weeks after that the general told Feigenbaum that his left arm would have to go.

"Oh dear me! But perhaps you would be kind enough to drop it over Israel."

But this time Fawzi was not to be moved.

"I'm afraid that this will not be possible."

"But why?" expostulated Feigenbaum.

"Because we have reason to believe you are trying to escape!"

A l Jolson told this story about his father.
"I bought my father an overcoat for $200, but I knew he'd be horrified at the cost so I told him I got it for $10! He rang me a few days later, very excited. 'Guess what! That coat you got me for $10 I just sold it for $25. Can you get me a dozen more?' "

J ack Levy went for dinner to Goldberg's restaurant and when he saw the tiny steak on his plate he burst into tears.

"What's the matter with you, Levy?" asks Goldberg.

"It's so sad," replied Ginsberg, weeping, "to think of it, a great big cow killed just to produce a tiny piece of meat like that."

M rs Ginsberg and Mrs Goldberg were discussing their sons.

"Is your son a good businessman?" asked Mrs Goldberg.

"Good? He's fantastic!" answered Mrs Ginsberg. "He's so dedicated he takes his secretary to bed every night in case he has an idea."

L ittle Izzy Levy was in the urinal, standing next to a very large black man. Looking down Izzy was astonished, and not a little jealous, to notice the magnificent size of his neighbour's equipment.

"Excuse me mister," he said, "but could you tell me how it is you've got such a magnificent member?"

"Simple, man, when I was a boy of ten, my mamma she tied a great brick to my member and for a whole month I walked about with it."

Izzy went home and at once called Sara, his wife. "Sara," he shouted, "cancel all visits and engagements. I'm not even going to work. I'm going to get myself a wonderful big shmock."

So Izzy tied a brick to his member and didn't leave the house for a month.

Eventually after the elapsed time, Sara said: "Well! Let's take a look and see how it's growing!"

Izzy opened his trousers, took a good look and said, "Well! We're halfway there! It's gone black!"

J oe and Molly had been married for sixty one years before they went to the rabbi to ask for a divorce.

"Divorce? Now? After all this time?" expostulated the rabbi. "Why?"

"Well," shrugged Joe, "we wanted to wait till the children died."

L ittle Moishe goes skating on the lake while his mother stands by, watching over him. Suddenly, through a crack in the thin ice, little Moishe vanishes.

"Oy veh!" shrieks his mother, "mine Moishe! In front of my very eyes."

Eventually a policeman comes, strips naked and dives into the icy water. Again and again, blue from cold, he dives in and eventually finds Moishe. The policeman manages to revive him, wraps him in his own clothes and rushes him to hospital where little Moishe eventually recovers.

Moishe's mother goes up to the policeman afterwards and says, "So? Where's his hat? He had a hat!"

Mendel saves up for years to buy a really fine tailor-made suit, his very first. But after he's been out in it for an hour or so, he notices there are things wrong with it. He goes back to the tailor.

"The arms are too long," says Mendel.

"No problem, just hold your arms out further and bend at the elbows."

"But the trouser legs are too long!"

"Right, no problem, walk with your knees bent."

"The collar's too high, it's halfway up the back of my head!"

"O.K., just poke your head out further."

So Mendel goes out into the world with his first tailor-made suit.

As he's passing a couple in the street, the woman says, "Look at that poor man! He must have had polio."

The man says: "But what a fine suit he's wearing."

G oldberg bought a champion greyhound and thought he would make a fortune at the dog track. But very sadly, the dog died before it could race.

A few months later Goldberg met Ginsberg who asked about the dog. "What! It died before it could make you a shekel? And such a famous dog! It's terrible."

"The dog made me a mint," said Goldberg.

"How so," enquired Ginsberg, astonished.

"Simple. I organised a raffle for the dog and I sold hundreds of tickets at £5.00 a time."

"Raffle a dead dog? And no complaints?"

"Sure, but only from the shmuck that won! So I gave him his £5.00 back!"

C ohen and Kelly were always arguing about
religion.

One day Cohen said, "What are you putting your
boy to?"

Kelly said, "I'll put him to the church."

Cohen said, "That's no life for a boy...no future."

Kelly said, "He might become a bishop."

Cohen said, "So! Living on charity."

Kelly still stuck to his point and said, "He could
become the Pope."

Cohen said, "Living in a tomb in Rome? What
life's that?"

Kelly got exasperated and said, "What would you
expect the boy to be? Jesus Christ himself?"

Cohen gave a grin and said, "Well...one of our
boys was."

A grandmother pushing a pram was stopped by an admiring stranger. "My goodness, is that your grandchild?"

"Sure! But you should see the photograph!"

S himon Peres, the Israeli Prime Minister, rang President Reagan:

"What's this about you sending an Arab into space?"

"Oh! Well, Shimon, don't worry, we'll send an Israeli next time..."

"You don't understand, Mr. President. I wasn't complaining. On the contrary, I congratulate you. But tell me, why stop at one?"

B eckie and Abie had been married fifty six years before they went to the rabbi to ask for a divorce.

"What?" he cried. "Divorce? After all these years? Why?"

Beckie slammed her fist on the table. "Enough is enough!" she cried.

G insberg and Goldberg are talking.

"You know the name of the biggest diamond in the world?"

"The Koh-i-noor."

"I might have known it was Jewish."

Morrie and Sara won £50,000 at the races. They couldn't believe their luck. But in the middle of the celebrations, Sara shouted: "Morrie! Morrie! But what about the begging letters?"

"What about them?" answered Morrie, "carry on sending them."

Where does a Jewish accountant keep the books?
In the kitchen — more handy for cooking.

How do you make a small fortune in Israel?
— Arrive with a large one.

Texans and Israelis are both big boasters. A Texan and an Israeli were pissing together over Brooklyn Bridge.

"Well, Yigal," drawled the Texan, "you sure can't complain, the water in the East River ain't too cold!"

"Na, Jim," replied the Israeli casually, "and it's not very deep either!"

A Texan Jew from Dallas was visiting Israel and, like all Texans, everything is bigger and better where he comes from.

He was being shown round an Israeli farm.

"What! You only have two hundred head of cattle? I have fifty thousand!"

"Well," said the Israeli farmer, "as you can see, I only have a few hundred acres."

"Mah God!" said the Texan, "why, I can get in my car and drive all day and I still won't reach my boundary fence!"

"I sympathise," said the Israeli, "I once had a car like that."

G insberg tried to sell Goldberg a painting.
      "But it's blank! It shows nothing!"
complained Goldberg.

"It's a fine work of art, an antique!" insisted Ginsberg. "It was painted by a close relative of Moses and shows the crossing of the Red Sea in Exodus."

"But there's nothing there! Where are the Israelites?" asked Goldberg.

"They've already crossed over."

Then where are the Egyptians?"

"They haven't arrived yet."

"So where's the water then?"

"Don't you remember, nudnik, the waters parted!"

M orrie Levy married a lovely black woman.
One day their boy came home from school
very disturbed.

"What's the matter, son?" asked Morrie.

"Am I black or a Jew?"

"Why?" asked his father. "You can be both."

"No," said his son, "you see, a boy at school's got
a radio he's selling for £5.00 and I don't know
whether to bargain with him or mug him!"

Mendel and Abie, partners in the dress business, are on holiday in Florida.

"Look at those wonderful flowers, Abie! What are they?"

"How should I know? Do I make hats or dresses?"

Isaac lives in the poorest district of Shplotsk and goes to the rabbi to complain about his condition.

"With eight children and only two rooms, how can I live in dignity?" asks Isaac.

"Well," says the rabbi, "try taking all the chickens from the yard into the house."

A week later Isaac told the rabbi that it had got even worse.

"Take the goats out of the back and put them in your bedroom," ordered the rabbi.

Again Isaac returned to the rabbi. "It's hell!" he said.

"Right," said the rabbi, "take the cows from the field and put them in the house."

Three days later, Isaac accosted the rabbi in the street. "I can't stand it any longer!"

So the rabbi told him to remove all the animals from the house immediately.

At the synagogue on the Sabbath, Isaac told the rabbi: "Thank you so much, it's wonderful. We have so much room!"

On the train between Pinsk and Minsk, Cohen observed the man seated opposite him with growing alarm. The man was whispering to himself and smiling; sometimes he would raise his hand and stop talking, then start again.

Cohen spoke: "Sorry to bother you, but is anything wrong?"

"No," replied the other, "I keep myself amused on train journeys by telling myself jokes."

"But why," persisted Cohen, "did you raise your hand?"

"Oh! I only do that to stop myself if I've heard the joke before."

M oishe Feigenbaum, a hit man for a notorious Jewish gang that once terrorised a small part of New York, was badly wounded in a shoot-out. Bleeding from several bullet wounds, he barely managed to crawl to his mother's house nearby.

"Mama! Mama! I'm hurt real bad!"

"Sit down and eat, Moishe. We can talk later!"

F ifteen minutes after the Titanic sank, Morrie and Louie find themselves on the same over-turned life raft. The water is freezing, sharks are cruising by and the raft is slowly sinking.

"Oh, well," said Louie, "it could have been worse."

"Worse? How could it be worse?" screamed Morrie.

"Well, we could have bought return tickets!"

" I had tea in a Jewish house yesterday."
"How did you know it was a Jewish house?"

"There was a fork in the sugar bowl."

T hree couples were killed in a coach crash on their holiday in Israel. They all went up to the gates of heaven where they were met by St Peter.

"What makes you think you belong here, Mr Cohen?" asked St Peter.

"Well, I go to synagogue regularly; I'm good to my employees and I look after my old mother."

St Peter replied: "In my book it says you're money mad because you married a woman called Penny, so down you go to the other place."

So down went the Cohens, but they told the other two couples what had happened.

Then it was the Levys' turn.

"What makes you think you belong up here?" asked St Peter.

"Well, I'm a regular worshipper at Synagogue, I'm a good father and I pay my bills on time."

"No," said St Peter, "in my book it says you're a drunk who married a girl called Sherry, so down you go."

So down went the Levys, who told the remaining couple what had happened.

Just before they were summoned in to St Peter, the last couple looked at each other and the man said, "Come on, Fanny, let's get out of here!"

D r Fortescue rang Ginsberg in a rage.
"That cheque you gave me just came back!"
"So did my arthritis!"

I t was a classic rags to riches story for Abie
Goldberg. He grew up in the poorest district
of London's East End, married a local girl, struggled
for years working twelve hours a day, seven days a
week, never took a holiday and eventually became
very wealthy, owning shipyards and a shipping
line. He had a beautiful house in Hampstead in
London, a villa in the south of France and a flat in
Miami. But success didn't spoil him. Once a year,
without fail, he goes back to Stepney to visit his wife
and kids.

"O.K.! It won't be long now!" said the rabbi as he circumcised the little boy.

Rabbi Cohen was most upset because the rich people in his flock were not generous enough. So next Sabbath day he prayed long and loud at the synagogue service that the rich should give more to the poor.

"Well, Rabbi," asked rich Mr Kaplan on leaving the synagogue, "was your prayer answered?"

"Half of it was," answered the rabbi. "The poor are willing to accept."

What's a psychiatrist?
A Jewish doctor who can't stand the sight of blood.

"May I park here?" asks Yossel, a newcomer to Israel, of the policeman in Tel-Aviv.

"No!" replied the policeman.

Yossel was perplexed. "But what about all those other cars?"

"They didn't ask."

Nathan Rosenbloom was on his way to market in Nuremberg with a duck under his arm.

He was stopped in the street by a Nazi brownshirt.

"Hey, Jew! Where do you think you're going?"

"I'm going to get some food in the market for my duck."

"What does he eat, your miserable duck?"

"Maize."

"Maize? Good Germans are dying of hunger and you Jews buy maize for your ducks?" He kicked Nathan about and went off.

A little later another Nazi stopped him.

"Where are you off to, Jewish dog?"

"To market, to get some food for my duck."

"What does he eat, this duck of yours?"

"Wheat."

"Wheat? Good wheat? German ex-soldiers are dying of hunger and you lousy Jews buy wheat for your ducks." He slapped Rosenbloom on the face and went off.

Soon another Nazi stopped Rosenbloom.

"Hey, swine!" he yelled, "where are taking that duck?"

"I'm going to market to get him some food."

"And what does your duck eat?"

"I'm not sure. I'll give it two pfennigs and it can get what it likes!"

Ginsberg visits Dr Goldberg.
   "Yeah, you're sick!"
"Not good enough. I want another opinion."
"O.K., you're ugly too!"

Ginsberg visits Dr Goldberg, a famous specialist.
"Well, what's wrong with me?"
"Nothing! You're fine!"
"Fine? What about my headaches?"
"I'm not worried about your headaches."
"Listen, Dr Goldberg, if you had any headaches, I wouldn't worry about them either!"

Old Morrie Feigenbaum was very old and suffering from a rare disease and he could only drink human milk.

"How can I get human milk?" Morrie asked the doctor.

"Well, Ruby Finkelstein's just had a baby, maybe she'll help."

So every day Morrie went to Ruby's house for his daily feed. Ruby was a dark-eyed, big-breasted lady who, in spite of herself, gradually became aroused as Morrie lapped at her ripe breasts. One day as he lay quietly sucking, she whispered to him, "Tell me, Mr Feigenbaum, do you like it?"

"Mmm, wonderful," he sighed.

"Is there," she hesitated, her lips parted, eyes aglow, "is there anything else you'd like?"

"As a matter of fact there is," murmured Morrie.

"What?" Ruby asked breathlessly.

Morrie licked his lips. "Maybe a little biscuit?"

I t was all Moses' fault!
If he'd made a right turn after crossing the Red Sea rather than a left turn, the Jews would have the oil and the Arabs would have the orange juice.

A poor Jew is walking down the street when he sees a rich funeral procession go by: black Rolls-Royces, lots of flowers, women in furs, a bronze-handled oak coffin. He shakes his head: "Now that's what I call living!"

In the religious instruction lesson the teacher asks the class: "Who wants to go to heaven?" All the children put their hands up, except for little Mendele. The teacher asks him why he doesn't want to go to heaven.

"Well, my father keeps saying, business has gone to hell' and I want to be where the business is."

A few Jewish sayings:

If people could hire other people to die for them then the poor could make a living.

If God lived on earth among men, his neighbours would break his windows.

If you tell the truth, you get beaten up.

God sends burdens...and shoulders.

F ather McManus begged Rabbi Levy to teach
him the principles of the Talmud.

"But you wouldn't understand the spirit behind
the Talmud," insisted the rabbi.

"Please try. I'm fascinated by it."

"All right, I'll give you a test. I'll ask you three
questions.

"First: Two men come down a chimney. One is
white, the other is black and filthy. Which one
washes himself?"

"Well, obviously, the dirty one," answers the
puzzled priest.

"No, it was the clean one because he looked at the
dirty one and thought he himself was as dirty,
whereas the dirty man saw the clean man and
decided he was clean as well, so did not wash
himself.

"Second question: Two men are coming down a
chimney. One is dirty, the other is clean. which one
washes himself?"

"Well, the clean one, of course."

"No, the dirty one, because he looks at himself,
compares his dirty condition to the clean man's and
washes himself.

"Third question: Two men are coming down a
chimney. One is clean, the other is filthy. Which one
washes himself?"

"Well, er, I don't know any more."

"See!" exulted the rabbi, "how could two men
come down the same chimney and one be dirty and
the other clean?"

B eckie yelled to Bennie, "It's the bank manager on the phone!"

"Yeah?" said Bennie, "what can I do for you?"

"You're £700 overdrawn, Mr Cohen."

"Psha!" said Bennie, "and what was my position last month?"

"Why, you were £250 in credit," said the bank manager.

"So!" snapped Bennie, "and did I ring you?"

Ginsberg ordered two bagels at Goldberg's restaurant. When they arrived he told Goldberg to change them for two blintzes. After eating them he got up to go.

"Wait!" shouted Goldberg. "You haven't paid for the blintzes."

"Don't try and catch me out," said Ginsberg, "I gave you two bagels for the blintzes."

"Yes, but you didn't pay for the bagels."

"Why should I pay for the bagels? I didn't eat them!"

I zzy and Yossel have been in business together for twenty-five years. Eventually Izzy's wife persuades him to take his first holiday. But on the very first day he feels he has to ring Yossel from Florida to find out how things are going.

"Izzy!" Yossel tells him, "the most terrible thing happened. Last night just after you'd gone, some thieves broke in and stole all the cash, the whole week's takings..."

"Yossel!" Izzy interrupts him firmly, "put it back!!"

In a Jewish village in Galicia, a Christian girl is found murdered. The Jews are petrified. They are bound to be blamed and there will be a terrible pogrom, or race riot.

Then, the rabbi, announces: "Wonderful news! We've just found out the girl was Jewish!"

Hymie and Abie were on the *Titanic* when it went down. They scrambled aboard a lifeboat and, out in the ocean, Abie started crying and wailing, making a terrible scene.

"What are you crying for?" asked Hymie. "It's not your boat."

Little Sarah swallowed fifty cents.

"Quick!" shouted her mother, "send for the doctor!"

"Doctor, rubbish!" shouted her father, "send for Hymie Goldberg! He can get money out of anybody!"

A schnorrer (Jewish beggar) called on Mrs Finklestein who took pity on him.

"Here, my man, you may have this," and she gave him a delicious slice of chollah (white bread). When he asked for more, he was given black bread.

"Is there no more chollah?" he expostulated.

"My man, chollah is very expensive."

"Lady, believe me, it's worth it!"

T wo old Jews meet in the street. Yossel stammers and Mendele limps.

"M-m-m-endele, I've g-g-g-ot an idea."

"Yes, what's that?"

"T-t-t-to stop lim-m-mping."

"Yes? Well?"

"You walk with one f-f-f-f-foot on the p-p-p-pavement and one f-f-f-foot in the g-g-g-gut-t-t-ter!"

"I see. And I've got a good idea how to stop stuttering."

"W-w-what is it?"

"Keep your bloody mouth shut!"

T he same Yossel met another friend.

"Yossel, how are you?"

"N-n-n-ot so w-w-w-onderful. I was t-t-turned down for a j-j-job."

"Oh? What was that?"

"As a n-n-n-news reader on the r-r-radio station. D-d-damn anti-Semites!"

Overheard in a men's urinal.
"Ah, I see you were circumcised by old Rabbi Feigenbaum."
"How on earth did you know?"
"Because you're pissing on my left foot.!"

Two rabbis were talking about how they made a little extra money on the side.
Rabbi Ginsberg said: "Well, I work in a battery factory standing near the conveyor belt."
"What can you do there?" asked Rabbi Goldberg.
"I just wave my hand as the batteries go by and say, 'I wish you a long life!' "

An old Jew asks his grandson: "Tell me, Hymie, explain this famous Einstein and his theory of relativity."

"Well, Grandpa," answers the youngster, "Einstein says that an hour sitting on a hot stove seems longer than an hour in a nice restaurant."

"Hmm," mused the old man, "and from this he makes a living?"

A son meets his father in a brothel.
"Dad! What are you doing here?"
"Should I bother your mother for thirty dollars?"

Hymie was on his way home when he found a perfectly good crutch lying abandoned in the road. Picking it up he hurried home and broke his wife's leg.

In the years of high inflation, two friends meet on the streets of New York.

"Well, how are you?"

"Terrible! I've been very ill. I've been away from work five months and it's cost me two thousand dollars on doctors and medicines."

"My god! Five years ago, on that kind of money, you could have been sick for a whole year!"

Business was so bad that Joe decided to end it all — so he went to a neighbour's house to gas himself.

Sarah and Molly were discussing their sex lives and Molly was astonished when Sarah told her she had just bought an 18-carat gold diaphragm studded with diamonds.

"Oy vey!" exclaimed Molly. "Whoever heard of such a thing?"

"What's so strange?" asked Sarah. "My Abie's ambition always was to come into money!"

A schnorrer managed to get to see Lord Rothschild.

"I have a fool-proof way for you to make half a million pounds."

"I see," said Rothschild, "and how do you propose I do that?"

"Well, I hear that when your daughter marries you'll give a dowry of one million pounds."

"That's correct."

"O.K.! I'll marry her for half a million."

A party of Jewish businessmen from Miami set off for a winter cruise in the Caribbean.

On New Year's Eve, the cabaret climaxed with a magician who announced a very special trick. As he waved his wand there was a huge explosion and the ship sank.

At dawn, Morrie Cohen is clinging to a piece of driftwood, rowing with one arm towards a distant shore. He sees another man hanging on to another piece of wood. As he approaches, Cohen yells:

"Hey! Are you the magician?"

"Yes."

"Big deal!!"

94